Merry
Christmas Lisa,
here's to many
magical moments and
wonderful memories.
Mom
1991

Whales & Dolphins

VIC COX

CRESCENT BOOKS

NEW YORK

This 1989 edition published by Crescent Books
distributed by Crown Publishers, Inc.,
225 Park Avenue South, New York, New York 10003

Printed and bound in Barcelona, Spain

ISBN 0-517-69092-6
hgfedcb

Cox, Vic.
    Whales and dolphins/Vic Cox.
        p.   cm.
    Includes index.
    ISBN 0-517-69092-6 (Crown)
    1. Cetacea   I. Title
QL737.C4C694   1989
599.5-dc20   89-1458
                                                          CIP

Written by: Vic Cox

Produced by: Ted Smart
Design by: Sara Cooper
Photo Research by: Edward Douglas
Editorial Assistance by: Seni Glaister

For rights information about the photographs in
this book please contact:

The Image Bank
111 Fifth Avenue, New York, N.Y. 10003

DEP. LEG. B-38.688-89

Whales & Dolphins

The beauty and genius of a work of art may be reconceived, though its first material expression be destroyed ... but when the last individual of a race of living things breathes no more, another heaven and another earth must pass before such a one can be seen again.

William Beebe, author, naturalist
and co-designer of the bathysphere.

Welcome to the Arctic

Borne on freezing flurries of wind, winter arrived early that year in the Arctic. The Inupiat Eskimo town of Barrow, Alaska, reported temperatures averaging 11 degrees below normal during the first three weeks of October. Sudden wind shifts hammered the mercury to 40 degrees below zero. Left undisturbed, seawater can freeze in such subzero weather in three hours. Rapidly forming coastal ice snaked toward the permanent ice pack floating a few miles out in the Beaufort Sea. Transforming the water into a crystalline prison, the ice encircled three young gray whales that had been feeding a few hundred yards offshore.

The grays, aged one to three years, were in a closing death trap when first spotted by Roy Ahmaogak, an Eskimo whaler from Barrow. They had only two breathing holes, the larger of which was about the size of a modest living room. Five miles of new ice blocked them from a channel through the offshore pack ice. If they could reach that slushy corridor before the shifting floes sealed it, the three whales would have a chance to get to the relatively open Bering Strait. From there it was a direct shot to the Chukchi Sea.

Even with a whale's highly efficient lungs--85 to 90 percent of their content is exchanged with each breath, compared to human lungs' 10 to 15 percent turnover--there was no way these marine mammals would hold their breath and swim five miles under the ice. When diving, some whales can stop respiration for perhaps as long as two hours, but grays (*Eschrictius robustus*) have a maximum known dive of about 12 minutes. Also, they do not seem to have the natural sonar that allows other kinds of cetaceans--the collective name of whales, porpoises and dolphins--to identify objects and navigate by the use of sound waves. Grays generally stick to coastlines and are believed to rely on memory when they migrate.

Left to the mercy of pack ice and nearby polar bears, the whales would have paid the ultimate price for their inexperience. Instead, humans intervened to attempt a rescue. It did not hurt that the grays became trapped only 14 miles from the sole television station within hundreds of miles. The news that three members of a well-known whale species were in a deadly white prison drew the attention of scientists, journalists and the President of the United States.

The whales were given two sets of names by their would-be rescuers. Biologists called the larger ones Crossbeak and Bonnet; the smallest, which was about 27 feet long, was tagged Bone, because it had scraped flesh off its rostrum, or beak. The Eskimos chose more scenic sobriquets, respectively naming them Poutu (ice hole), Siku (ice) and Kannick (snowflake). Photos of Eskimo hunters petting the game grays made the world's press.

As word of the whales' plight spread, Operation Breakthrough was mounted under the aegis of the U.S. National Oceanic and Atmospheric Administration. In the end, the two whales that survived the three week struggle were freed by an international coalition of strange allies: Eskimo whalers with chain saws, environmental groups stoking the media fires, de-icing machine entrepreneurs from Minnesota, an Alaska National Guard helicopter armed with a five-ton concrete ice crusher, a pipeline firm's 11 ton ice-breaking "Archimedian Screw Tractor" and two Soviet ice breakers.

To avoid startling the grays in the wrong direction under the ice, the heavy equipment worked farthest from the animals. Eskimos cut a trail of more than 60 breathing holes to link up with the path punched by the helicopter through two-foot-thick ice. The de-icing machines kept open each new hole and provided the whales with an acoustic signal to guide their slow advance. Sound travels through water five times faster than through air, and the grays, as is true of whales small and large, have fine hearing.

Meanwhile, the Soviet ships plowed through a massive pressure ridge of ice while the tractor helped clear the way to the ridge. Fortunately, the weather co-operated and kept the ice pack at bay during the final eight days of the ordeal. Later some would call it a media circus and a misuse of resources--the cost of Operation Breakthrough was estimated at around $1 million--others found the co-operative venture inspiring and even slightly redemptive given the long, bloody exploitation of whales by humans.

As is often the case with whale rescues, no one could be certain the survivors would make it back to the relative safety of the open sea. Arctic sharks and orcas are the natural predators of various whale species. Then, though the two grays looked healthy and fat to biologists despite beaks rubbed raw by the ice, they still had to swim nearly 6,000 miles to reach their home waters--the placid mating and calving lagoons of western Baja California. Crossbeak and Bonnet faced one of the longest known mammal migrations in the natural world. But they had most likely done it before and at least now, they had another chance.

≈

Baleen Whales

Migration to escape winter is a primordial pattern for many whale species, particularly those that feed on tiny crustaceans and small fish in the nutrient-rich waters of the polar seas. These are the "mustached" whales, the branch of the cetacean family known as the Mysticeti. They range in size from the pygmy right whale (*Caperea marginata*) with a maximum length of 20 feet, to the female blue (*Balaenoptera musculus*), with a pre-whaling era maximum estimated at over 100 feet.

The Mysticeti comb tiny organisms from the water with baleen, a series of stiff but flexible vertical plates with a fringed edge. The plates hang from the interior of the upper jaw, the rostrum, in closely packed layers. When the whale's tongue forces water out of its mouth, the baleen, which is made of the same substance that forms human fingernails and hair, efficiently strains out hundreds of pounds of tiny animals at a time. Under the name of whalebone, baleen was once used as stays in ladies' corsets and dresses and as buggy whips and umbrella ribs, among other common items.

Some baleen whales, like the Arctic bowhead (*Balaena mysticetus*) or the northern and southern rights (*Eubalaena glacialis*) usually feed by leisurely skimming through surface swarms of organisms. Their gigantic heads occupy nearly one-third of the whales' total body length. Raising elongated, narrow rostrums just above the water, their mouths deploy the long fringe of keratin strands--the bowhead's baleen plates can grow to 15 feet--to full advantage. The ventral or throat grooves swell to hold the water. There may be as many as 400 baleen plates on each side of the upper jaw. Some bowheads skim-feed in groups of a dozen or more in a wedge-shaped formation reminiscent of geese flying south. Researchers think this boosts their foraging efficiency.

Other baleen whales are known as gulpers, because they prefer taking a quick bite to lingering over a meal. Among these are the largest animals on the planet: the 150 ton blue and the 88 foot long, 80 ton fin (*Balaenoptera physalus*) whales. Their enormous throat pouches are grooved with accordion-like pleats that allow vast and rapid expansion as the mammals lunge open-mouthed after their prey. The adult blue whale's mouth can hold an estimated 70 tons of food and water in this manner.Its hundreds of fine baleen plates gather the shrimp-like crustaceans, or krill, it feeds on almost exclusively. Krill are only two inches long, which is fortunate since the esophagus of the blue and fin whales is about four inches wide.

Fins, which have more and coarser baleen than the blues, filter out the larger planktonic animals. They eat small fish that travel in shoals as well. Due to the characteristic throat pleats, which also adorn sei, Bryde's and minke, this group of whales has been christened the rorquals, after the Norwegian words for tube, or furrowed, whale.

When conditions demand, there is more finesse to rorqual fishing than the gulping method implies. While all of these whales are agile, active hunters, some have developed special techniques. Fins, which are the only known asymmetrically colored cetacean species, have been reported using the large white area on their right side to help confuse and concentrate schools of capelin and herring. Bunching their prey fish together makes for a more filling gulp, or so the theory goes. Fins frequently hunt in pairs.

Better documented is a feeding technique called bubble netting which has been termed characteristic of humpbacks (*Megaptera novaeangliae*) in the North Pacific. As it rapidly circles below a school of small fish, the whale releases bursts of air, which form a noisy barrier of bubbles as they ascend. A glittering circle some 30 to 100 feet in diameter corrals the prey long enough for a savvy cetacean to lunge up through the middle. Such bubble nets may also be U- or V-shaped, with the whale barrelling in from the open end, jaws agape.

A different version of bubble netting has been seen among some North Atlantic humpback groups. A whale expels a cloud of large bubbles under a shoal, which rises to the surface en masse, reaching a diameter of up to 25 feet. The humpback swims after the cloud, lunging open-mouthed through the center. Presumably, the massed bubbles concentrate and distract the fish as well as hide the predator's approach.

Individual humpbacks studied off Cape Cod, Massachusetts, had their own twists to the basic bubble method. Researchers from the Cetacean Research Unit of the Gloucester Fisherman's Museum, who also named the whales, reported that Cat's Paw liked to surface in a vertical position on an edge of the bubble cloud, raising herself out of water to her flippers. Her mouth would be closed, ventral pleats tight, and eyes open. As she slipped down, her mouth opened, funneling in prey; she reappeared in the cloud 15 or 20 secounds later with a wide-mouthed lunge. Binoc, on the other hand, was one of several whales who breached. Its huge form rose one-third out of the water and smashed the surface. Then Binoc would blow a bubble cloud and take whatever it held in a horizontal lunge. Other area humpbacks chose to slam the surface with their flukes, a behavior known as lobtailing, before releasing clouds. Observers speculated that lobtailing and breaching may have stunned the small fish the whales sought.

In comparison with the rorquals and humpbacks, the gray has downright grubby table manners. It is the only baleen whale that routinely feeds off the coastal sea floor, though there is some evidence that bowheads may also suction animals from the bottom. Shallow craters and serial gouges in the mud mark grays' foraging sites. The gray has 140 to 180 thick, yellowish baleen plates along each side of the upper jaw. Its coarse bristles, which are usually no more than 16 inches long, sweep clean blades of eel grass and kelp strands as well as seperating animals from the mud.

Swimming sideways to the bottom, the whale sucks up dense aggregations of amphipod crustaceans and the mud they live in, expelling the muck as it heads toward the surface. The gray's sparse and rudimentary throat grooves seem to aid the tongue's suctioning movements as it swims. These grooves do not expand as with the rorquals and humpbacks. There is some evidence that when grays disturb the bottom sediment they help open up the habitat to new residents, thus maintaining a healthy amphipod community.

≈

Toothed Whales

The cetacean family tree's other main branch is the Odontoceti, the toothed whales. This branch has generally smaller whales than the baleens, but because they include dolphins and porpoises, their kind are more numerous. While the Mysticeti comprise 10 species--11 if you divide right whales into northern and southern species, as some authorities do--by current count there are approximately 80 toothed species. They range from the 60-foot male sperm whale (*Physeter macrocephalus*) to the 5-foot La Plata River dolphin (*Pontoporia blainvillei*) and live in the depths of the sea or the shallows of freshwater rivers.

Given the diversity of cetaceans, it is not surprising that researchers still argue over proper taxonomy of some large and small whales. Confusion and disagreement are probably inevitable, because many species are classified from skeletal remains of a few individuals discovered on far-flung beaches.

This is particularly true of the beaked and bottlenosed whales, the Ziphiidae. Longman's beaked whale (*Mesoplodon pacificus*), for instance, is known only from two skulls--one of which was found in Australia in 1926 and the other in Somalia in 1955. Nor will cetologists foreclose the possibility that there are species yet to be discovered in the oceans that blanket more than 70 percent of the Earth's surface.

Even less likely to be settled is the confusion that arises over the common labeling of some toothed cetaceans as either dolphin or porpoise. While *Tursiops truncatus*, so familiar from films, oceanaria and television shows, is generally known as the bottlenose dolphin, there are a few who call it the bottlenose porpoise. Many popular and scientific writers tend to use the terms interchangeably; a few strictly observe the taxonomic distinctions that split the generally long-beaked Delphinidae, with their cone-shaped teeth, from the true porpoise. The latter are members of the Phocoenidae family, which usually have small, flat, spade-shaped teeth and no visible beak.

Tooth shape is of little help in identifying wild animals at sea. Dall's porpoise (*Phocoenoides dalli*) have such small teeth that they are hidden by their gums. Besides, if you are close enough to inspect a whale's teeth, you probably have other things on your mind--such as getting out of the water intact. As natural, and wisely cautious, as is that reaction, there is no reason to believe that people are part of any odontocete's diet.

Head shape is generally different between dolphins and porpoises, but there are exceptions. Risso's dolphin (*Grampus griseus*) and the pilot whale (*Globicephalus melaena*) are round headed and essentially beakless. Both are certified members of the dolphin family. Likewise, size is no real family indicator. The 30-foot orca, or killer whale (*Orcinus orca*), is the largest delphinid.

Toothed whales make their living hunting very fast prey, such as squid. The soft bodied cephalopod is a mainstay of most species, including the deep-diving sperm whale, which can grow to 60 feet long and weigh in at 50 tons. Researchers aboard whaling vessels have found sperms with as many as 15,000 pairs of squid beaks in their stomachs. Most of these are deep-water squid less than three feet long and weighing under two pounds. An investigator calculated that a sperm whale population of approximately 1.25 million alone would consume around 100 million tons of squid a year. These predators also eat different kinds of fish, such as the speedy barracuda, the albacore tuna and various sharks.

One indicator of a sperm whale's diving ability comes from the stomach of one killed in 1969 off the coast of South Africa after it had been submerged for nearly an hour and a half. Inside it, whalers found two small sharks that lived only on the sea floor, which in this area was over 10,000 feet down.

This is indirect evidence, but there are instances where sperms have become entangled in deep-sea communications cables and drowned. The greatest depth at which this has happened was 3,720 feet off the South American coast between Peru and Ecuador. That deep down, the 47-foot bull sperm in question would have had to withstand a pressure of 1,680 pounds per square inch. It was no consolation to the whale, but his dive made it into the *Guinness Book of World Records*.

In comparison to its body size, the lungs of a sperm or any other whale are relatively small. So how can a whale resist the terrible pressure of a deep dive and still be able to rise quickly to the surface? If human divers make a rapid ascent, nitrogen bubbles form in their bloodstream, creating an often lethal condition called "the bends".

Cetaceans actually take in very little air on a dive, allowing the pressure to compress their lungs and force that air into their windpipes and extensive nasal passages. Thick membranes contain the nitrogen gas bubbles, preventing most of the exchange to tissues and blood that occurs when humans scuba dive. Because whales are able to store twice as much oxygen in their muscles as we can, they have normal muscle function on a dive for a longer period. If, as seems probable, whales can also reduce their heart rate and restrict blood flow, such physiology would reduce oxygen need and help prevent the chilling of these warm-blooded mammals.

An insulating layer of fat tissue, called blubber, is what whales traded for hair when their ancestors left the land to return to mother ocean around 55 million years ago. Though some vestigial hairs remain, blubber is the main barrier against the heat-sucking cold of the sea. On Arctic residents, like the bowhead, the blubber coat is more than 28 inches thick. Adult sperm whales, which stay mostly in tropical and temperate waters, have a foot-deep layer of blubber under thick, corrugated skins.

Blubber has other functions, such as food storage and buoyancy regulation, and may help the skin trim water turbulence as the whale swims. It also melts to various grades of oil when heated in rendering vats. The economics of this biological fact built a huge, multinational whaling industry that eventually reduced most whale species to remnants.

While many toothed whales have functional jaws that allow them to catch and tear (but not chew) their prey, sperm jaws apparently don't work that way. The 18 to 25 massive teeth in the lower jaw only erupt when the whale is about twice its birth length of 12 to 14 feet, well after it has been weaned. The upper teeth rarely descend from the gums, leaving sockets into which the lower ones fit. Most of the squid found in their stomachs show no tooth marks. The discovery of stones, crabs, sand, glass fishing buoys and even a shoe or two in their stomachs suggests to some observers that sperms occasionally plow the ocean bottom with their slender lower jaws.

There is much speculation but few answers on how sperm whales actually catch their meals. One theory holds that they may lure prey into their mouths after somehow masticating luminescent organisms that, in turn, attract the hapless squid. Another theses argues that sperm vocalization abilities include the capacity for producing sound waves intense enough to stun or kill their food. More on this later.

Like the sperm whale, orcas use their large, conical teeth on fish and squid, which make up the bulk of their diet. But orcas are also called killer whales, because they are among the few cetaceans known to hunt and eat other marine mammals, including the sperm and blue whales. When 40 to 52 interlocking teeth are commanded by a 30-foot, 8-ton male orca, who may be leading a family group, or pod, of from three to more than 20 like-minded predators, instant respect is the rule. Yet there are reports of orcas feeding on fish in the vicinity of potential mammalian prey--like baleen whales, porpoises and sea lions--without raising alarm.

Orcas are wide-ranging, opportunistic carnivores with a highly developed social structure apparently based on pods. An example of orca co-operative hunting comes from the waters off St. John's, Newfoundland, where four killers circled herring with vigorous splashing and noise-making displays to corral the fish. Scientists on the scene recorded underwater sounds and vocalizations that they thought aided the orcas in identifying and herding their prey.

Fishermen off Norway and New Zealand have reported similar episodes of orcas herding fish and dolphins into milling circles. Then the hunters took turns at feeding. While a few went in for the kill, the rest of the pod circled the prey, keeping them bunched for as long as possible.

Sometimes an attack by a pod of orcas takes on the appearance of a human military operation. A well-known example comes from the pages of Captain Robert F. Scott's Antarctic expedition diary. A group of six or seven orcas were swimming near the edge of the ice where Scott's ship was moored. To film them, H.L. Ponting, the expedition photographer, positioned his camera on an ice floe to which were tethered two sled dogs. Naturally, the orcas disappeared. Suddenly, Ponting lost his balance when the floe heaved as it was struck from below. A resounding series of booms could be heard as the whales repeatedly battered the 2.5 foot thick ice. It split into fragments as Ponting freed the dogs, gathered his equipment and jumped from floe to floe. As man and dogs fled to safety, the orcas raised their heads six or eight feet above water--a behavior called spyhopping--to locate their targets. They did not give chase. Since that frightening but instructive encounter in 1911, others have reported orcas successfully forcing seals off the ice in the same manner.

Co-operative hunting methods are not unique to orcas, though their strength, speed and adaptability leave lasting impressions. Other toothed whales often hunt together, particularly the coastal bottlenose dolphin. This author witnessed three of these dolphins herding mullet against an islet near the mouth of Crystal River in north central Florida. Using a slight curve in the mud bank as a wall, two animals came in splashing from one direction while the third approached quietly from the opposite side. Fish launched themselves into the air, fleeing the noisemakers. Then the pair split up about 12 feet from the islet, with one dolphin moving into position between the now stationary opposing two. Availing themselves of the bay's geography, the dolphins had created a triangular fish trap. As if on signal, the animal at the apex rushed toward the center, slapping the surface with its tail. The other dolphins converged--and half a dozen silver-gray fish exploded from the water in what must have been, for some, a vain attempt at escape.

Large schools of around 200 bottlenose dolphins have been sighted forming a single line to herd fish in South African coastal waters. A small group on the periphery broke off and speeded up, swinging around after their sprint to close with the main rank of hunters. As the groups merged, the two orderly lines dissolved into a frenzy of catch-as-catch-can feeding.

Dall's porpoises have dozens of very small teeth that are separated by horny ridges known as "gum teeth." They also have a ridged pad on the upper jaw tip that is thought to assist in grasping soft-bodied animals like squid and octopus. Stomachs full of deepsea fish, such as lantern fishes and smelt, as well as an appetite for squid are evidence of the porpoise's deep-diving abilities.

These porpoises are among the most rapid of cetaceans, with speeds reported to reach 33 miles per hour. When swimming this fast and lifting their heads above water to breathe, a characteristic, and unique, rooster-tail of spray is created. Another unusual feature is that sometimes these animals swim in single file, head to tail. Such a sighting was reported in 1956 off San Pedro, California, of a group of Dall's porpoises numbering around 100.

~

Beaked Whales

The open ocean beaked whales boast some of the most unusually shaped teeth among the odontocetes, yet their function is basically unknown. Some shapes have been compared to the leaf of the ginkgo tree or that of a flattened onion. Moreover, there are not that many teeth to analyze. The majority of species have from a few pairs to just two individual teeth, but these teeth can be marvelous adornments. The adult male strap-toothed whale *(Mesoplodon layardii)* has boarlike tusks on each side of his lower jaw that may become a foot long and wrap around the upper jaw. At that length, they restrict the whale from opening wide its mouth. How he captures and swallows the squid that are his staple diet is puzzling, though he may simply suck them up. The female strap-toothed's teeth apparently do not erupt through her gums.

Few of the female sex among 18 species in the beaked whale family have visible teeth, though there is usually some dentition in the lower jaw. The only species in which both sexes have a full complement of functional teeth is Shepherd's beaked whale *(Tasmacetus shepherdi)*. This animal, which can grow to at least 30 feet, has 17 to 21 pairs of small, sharp teeth in its upper jaw and 18 to 27 pairs in the lower jaw. The female does not have the male's pair of long, strong teeth on the tip of the pointed lower jaw. From analysis of one stranded specimen in southern Argentina, these whales are thought to eat various fish, small crabs and squid.

Small whale fisheries in Japan and Norway have hunted Baird's beaked whale, Cuvier's beaked whale, and the North Atlantic bottlenose whale, but science has only a passing acquaintance with most of the Ziphiidae. Of these rare beaked and bottlenose whales, perhaps the most common is Cuvier's *(Ziphius cavirostris)*. This slope-faced whale has only two teeth, which protrude slightly from a lower jaw that juts beyond the upper one. The shape, light color and relatively small size of its rostrum give it the other popular name of goosebeak whale. Reaching a length of 23 feet and a weight of five tons, it apparently inhabits all the deep oceans, save for those in the polar regions. Squid and deep-dwelling oceanic fish are its main prey.

French naturalist Baron Georges Cuvier first described the whale that bears his name from a skull found near Marseilles in 1804. It seems to strand more often than other beaked whales and has been found on beaches in Japan and Hawaii, along the U.S. West and East coasts, and in the Caribbean, England, Spain and Italy as well as France. Despite the relative abundance of dead specimens, there are few recorded observations of how Cuvier's beaked whale lives in the wild.

Even sparser information is available on Blainville's

beaked whale *(Mesoplodon densirostris)*, or the dense-beaked whale, as it is sometimes labelled. It is also a deep-water resident but seems to prefer the warmer climes of the world's tropical seas. The male's thick, stair-stepped lower jaw has a single tooth growing out of the middle on both sides. Such a location is no help in catching the slippery squid on which the Blainville's and most other beaked whales feed. However, the palates of these cetaceans are ridged and may aid in holding captured squid.

The Blainville's canine-like tooth is missing in adult females and juveniles, who have the same shaped lower jaw as the males. Since a few inches of teeth are visible, they may be a symbol of male sexual maturation, but it is difficult to imagine rival males trying to scrape each other with them, as some researchers suggest.

≈

Unicorn of the Arctic

The mystery of how different toothed whales feed sharpens when a strangely mottled cetacean thrusts its 8-foot-long, hollow, hornlike tooth into sight. The male narwhal *(Monodon monoceros)* has only one tooth, which grows in a forward spiral out of the left side of its head. If the tooth is a weapon, as has been theorized, it is an unwieldly one for an animal no more than 16 feet long and weighing about 3,000 pounds. Females rarely grow such a tusk and generally have no functional teeth. A deep-water animal that is most common in the circumpolar High Arctic region, the narwhal eats shrimp, squid, crabs, cod, halibut, and other small fish. They crush prey in their jaws and swallow them whole. These "sea unicorns," as they have been called, are quick, agile swimmers despite having no dorsal fin.

The tooth's function has long been cause for curiosity—and superstition. European royalty once believed that the horn's material could neutralize poisons, so it was in great demand for drinking cups. Even after that myth wore thin, narwhal teeth had high decorative value. A British explorer once sent Elizabeth I a tusk to complement her imperial robes. The throne of Denmark's kings at Rosenborg Castle, Copenhagen, incorporates tusks as its upright supports.

Available scientific evidence indicates that the tooth, while performing no anti-poison function, is useful in ritual fighting over females. It has been likened to the horns and antlers of some land grazers who make impressive displays (including the butting of heads) to gain sexual dominance over rivals. Male narwhals take the ritual so far as to cross tusks and inflict wounds. Canadian studies confirm that narwhals have a social pecking order based on which has the longest tooth.

Sensing the Water World

Though not all species have been tested, cetologists are confident that whales use sound more than sight to survive in the water world. If you consider the freshwater dolphins, who are born with small, weak eyes or no eyes at all, this seems an obvious conclusion. However, large and small dolphins have fine eyesight, as demonstrated by captive animals who accurately launch themselves through hoops suspended in air or take fish from the mouth of a trainer, an orca's length above the pool. In the latter case, the trainer is literally betting his head on the orca's depth perception and visual acuity, not to mention its mood of the moment.

Living in seawater, which transmits sound waves more efficiently than does air, places a premium on a whale's ability to hear--and enlarges our terrestrial concept of that sense. Coastal waters are often murky from river discharge or the sewage and pollution of human aggregations and activities. Even the clearest open ocean water filters light so that the last feeble rays cannot penetrate beyond 1,600 feet; some cetaceans seek food beyond this boundary.

Finding and identifying individual prey is a key problem for rapidly swimming predators. The solution evolved by dolphins, porpoises and other toothed whales is to locate objects by bouncing pulsed waves of sound off them and reading the echo. This process is called echolocation.

Toothed whales are capable of producing a wide spectrum of sounds, which scientists divide principally into types of clicks and whistles. Virtually all odontocetes studied have individually unique phonations, known as "signature whistles," which help them identify each other. Some whistles or tones can be detected by the unaided human ear. Whalers called the beluga, or white whale *(Delphinapterus leucas)*, the "sea canary," because of its astonishing repertoire of vocalizations. People on the surface have reported hearing sounds that reminded them of bird calls, mooing, deep sighing, teethgnashing, the shaking of a tin tray, and musical glasses being played badly. With the invention of the underwater microphone, science gained access to much more acoustical information on whales, but the descriptions dropped in literary imagery.

Echolocation relies on an intense beam of clicks over high frequencies that bounce back from objects, enabling the whale to form an acoustical picture of its surroundings. Humans employ the same principle of echo-formed images with radar and sonar. Experiments with blindfolded captive bottlenose dolphins, which started in the late 1950s, have documented the remarkable sophistication of this natural form of active sonar. The captives have been able to detect a 10-percent difference in the diameter of metallic spheres; various shapes and thicknesses of objects; a 3/10 inch variation in wall thickness of cylinders; and to discriminate among aluminum, bronze and steel cylinders of equal dimensions. One test of a bottlenose tried to measure the maximum distance at which it could locate a target. The dolphin found a tangerine-sized object 400 yards away with extremely intense bursts of clicks.

Another experiment, involving the tracking of a live fish in a tank festooned with hydrophones, revealed that dolphins have hearing so acute it acts like passive sonar. Without using any clicks, they can track and catch prey under certain conditions by listening for its sounds. Since the ocean is filled with noises from physical and biological sources, fine hearing alone is not enough for a predator. Researchers now believe active and passive sonar abilities combine to form the type of echolocation toothed whales possess.

There is some scientific consensus on how whales generate and direct echolocation clicks. The main school of thought holds that the sounds are produced by recycling air in nasal passages below the blowhole and are focused into a beam by the anatomy and oil reservoir in the animal's melon, or forehead. The echoes bounce back and are channeled by oil-filled passages in the lower jaw to the inner ear. This system corresponds to the anatomy of the bottlenose dolphin and many other delphinids.

An opposing, largely European-held view is that sounds originate in the cetacean larynx, just as they do in other mammals, and hearing is through the tiny ear canals. This minority theory admits that whales do not have vocal chords but argues that vibrations from the larynx could be transmitted to the rostrum through certain muscles. The sound beams theorized for this form of echolocation would be emitted from both the melon and throat regions. Such a dual-beam sonar has been claimed in some freshwater dolphins, but so far supportive evidence is weak.

If all this sounds like a tempest in some scientific teacup, consider one of the most intriguing, and potentially important, ideas to surface from echolocation research: "the Big Bang Theory." It holds that toothed whales can produce sound waves intense enough to immobilize, even kill, prey within a certain distance. If a dolphin can find a small object more than a football field's length away from it, could not such intense sounds also stun prey swifter than the predator? Two Soviet researchers suggested in 1963 that the sperm whale employs the oil-filled case in its great nose, which is used in echolocation, to do just that. This would explain why there are few tooth marks on squid, particularly those found in the bellies of sperm whales with deformed jaws. The idea re-emerged in papers published in the 1970s and 1980s by Soviet, European and American cetologists, among them Dr. Kenneth Norris, a professor of natural history at the University of California at Santa Cruz.

A former oceanarium curator, Norris is a pioneer in dolphin echolocation studies. He is also a point man for the argument that echolocating sounds start in nasal airways and are focused by the melon. Being able to direct sound beams at targets of varying distance by muscular changes in the melon is crucial to the big bang effect--what Norris likes to call ensonification. But while the same mechanism generates the echolocation beam and the proposed stun beam, current research indicates that there are two different kinds of sound involved.

Echolocation employs beams of high-frequency sound pulses. The stun beam seems to rely on long, low-frequency pulses five times stronger than echolocation clicks. Both sound beams may be emitted simultaneously. Norris now believes that because the stun pulse lasts up to 800 times longer than the echolocation click, the sound builds up an overload in a fish's system that can kill it. If correct, his analysis places a sonic weapon in the melon of every toothed whale. But Norris is the first to point out that the key evidence is still missing: researchers have yet to record a whale using its hypothesized beam to kill a fish, though humans have killed anchovies in Santa Cruz harbor by mimicking the sound.

Like many explanations of cetacean behavior, the Big Bang Theory was launched by little more than anecdotal information and deductive logic. Observers of both wild and captive dolphins noted fish being chased that suddenly became unco-ordinated and disoriented, or just went limp, and the pursuing whale gobbled them up. One diver in the Bahamas, who had managed to get close to a school of dolphins that was accompanied by four large bonito, saw some whales pointing at bottom fish a few yards away. Then he heard them making very loud echolocation sounds. When a fish went limp or started to vibrate, one of the bonito darted in and ate it. That story suggests ensonification, but it also raises a question: if the dolphins are so smart, why were they feeding the bonito?

Norris is particularly fascinated with dolphins' social relationships in light of each possibly controlling an equally powerful weapon. "We see peacefulness both between and within the dolphin societies we look at," he says. The question is, does this general peacefulness result from the built-in equalizer all dolphins presumably have or, some other factor? In plucking at strands of this puzzle, Norris and his colleagues discovered examples of what he calls "echolocation manners" among captive spinner dolphins. "We've found that they almost never ensonified each other with intense sound."

Motion pictures of the captive animals also illustrate a

major rule of dolphin society: it's rude, perhaps dangerous, for dolphins to face each other. Adults rarely do so. Dolphin schools are organized so that individuals swim parallel to one another. "Even a slight motion--the smallest tip of the head--will cause the other animals to move," says Norris. "It is a negative signal to point, even slightly, at another animal, and this rule is what steers dolphin schools." Young dolphins often point at their mothers and blast away. But they also are learning to control sound production as well as the rules of dolphin society, Norris says, so harmful intensity is as unlikely as it is unintentional.

In an almost featureless environment, it might seem necessary for all whales to rely on sound to visualize their world as well as to communicate with each other. Yet there is scant evidence that baleen whales can echolocate. Grays, humpbacks and minkes have, on occasion, been reported making click sounds and various whistles. Several kinds of sounds have been recorded from blues and right whales. But few will risk their reputations to claim baleen echolocation on such fragmentary evidence.

Evidence of baleen whales using sounds to communicate among themselves is much stronger. Studies of right whales breeding in southern Argentina found their sounds helped keep individuals, especially mothers and calves, in physical proximity, and that they grew more elaborate the more active and complicated the social behavior became. This suggested some exchange of information, even if the content was ambiguous. Similarly, the blue has a low-frequency call that, under ideal conditions, may be heard for thousands of miles. To many cetologists, such capability seems designed for reaching out and keeping in touch with other blue whales.

Humpbacks are now famous for singing long, complex "songs" while on breeding grounds in Hawaii and Bermuda. It turns out that they also sing just before, and possibly during, migration to the tropics. Though the meaning of a repeated pattern of sounds, which is what is meant by a song, is unclear, some authorities think it a call to the female, since it seems solely a male performance. A remarkable feature is that all males in the same whale population sing basically the same song, which varies slightly from one mating season to the next until it is a completely new song. Modification of group singing behavior is virtually unknown outside of humans and has been interpreted as a sign of intraspecies communication.

~

Whale Adaptability

Whales are complex animals capable of adapting to many different conditions and habitats--from the polar pack ice to the sunless sea bed, from murky rivers to shallow coastal lagoons. Some, especially the toothed whales, live and hunt in social groups; others, like the blue and the humpback, individually forage the oceans. Orcas are seemingly at home in nearly any body of water. And some whales are residents of highly circumscribed habitats. The Chinese river dolphin (*Lipotes vexillifer*) lives only in the middle and lower regions of the Quintangjiang and Yangtze rivers. Freshwater dolphins are, almost by definition, restricted to certain rivers, but here again the generalization runs up against cetacean adaptability. The stocky little La Plata River, or franciscana, dolphin lives in salty, brackish shallows along the south Atlantic coastlines of Argentina, Uruguay and Brazil. It is unlikely to be found up the river for which it is named.

Migration from cold to warm waters in both hemispheres is a common way of handling changing climatic conditions in different marine habitats. As fall ends in either hemisphere, fins and blues swim from polar feeding grounds toward the Equator, where they mate and give birth. Even though they are among the best researched baleens, their migration routes remain a secret. North Pacific humpbacks make the winter journey from Alaska to Hawaii for mating; from the waters around Greenland and Iceland, North Atlantic humpbacks go to the Caribbean for their amorous rendezvous. During approximately six months of migration and mating, these rorquals take little if any nourishment. They live off the energy stored in their blubber.

Distance seems no obstacle for even a medium-sized baleen like the gray whale. It spends summer and a few fall months gorging in Arctic waters, then cruises 5,000 to 6,000 miles south to winter in the lagoons of Baja California. Unlike the rorquals, the gray probably snacks en route and during its warmer-water interlude. It has recently been discovered that not all southbound grays migrate all the way to Baja. Instead they congress off British Columbia, Washington, Oregon and California. In the milder climate the adult grays mate or, if pregnant, females give birth and nurse calves. It is an ancient rite: whales with an anatomy nearly identical to today's grays were swimming in California's bays more than 20 million years ago.

The official population estimate of this whale species is more than 20,000; not bad for an animal that commercial whaling has pushed to the edge of extinction twice in this century. Before taking bows for finally stopping the killing of grays (except for subsistence purposes) in 1949, we should note that the whale's Atlantic population is now history and the remnants of a western Pacific population are so seldom seen off Korea that they, too, are supposed extinct.

~

Commercial Whaling

Seafaring men have taken whale lives long before history was kept in written form. Native Americans on both coasts, Eskimos, Stone Age Norsemen, and the Basques of western Europe all whaled. The Basques, by about AD 1000, had an industry efficient enough to decimate the right whale population in the Bay of Biscay. By the mid-1500s, Basque whalers had crossed the Atlantic and were whaling rights and bowheads along the coast of what is now the Canadian province of Labrador. In the 1600s, the demand for whale oil and whalebone sent the Dutch, British, Germans and French after whales in the European Arctic as populations of coastal animals were whittled down.

Yankee whaling was launched soon after settlements took root in New England. By 1720, European whalers, particularly the British, joined the Americans off the frigid coasts of Canada and Greenland to slaughter the oil-rich bowheads and right whales. When they eventually grew scarce, humpbacks, grays and any other large whale that could be caught were killed and butchered and their blubber melted. Sperm whales, whose meat is held unpalatable outside of Japan and Indonesia but whose case oil is the finest in the world, became the Yankee whalers' prime target between 1820 and 1860. Then the widening use of less expensive, easy-to-get petroleum sent most whaling industries into a tailspin. However, the petroleum revolution proved a respite rather than a pardon for the great whales. In the twentieth century, sperm oil has been used as a lubricant for automobile transmissions.

Up to the end of the last century, whaling was restrained by a technology based on hand-held harpoons and vessels propelled by wind and oars. At least this allowed the faster swimming (and quicker sinking) rorquals to avoid wholesale carnage. In the latter half of the nineteenth century, wooden sailing ships started converting to steam power and the explosive grenade harpoon was invented. Then the baleens' Antarctic feeding grounds were discovered.

The result was the advent of no-holds-barred modern commercial whaling, an approach that systematically decimated whole species and eventually doomed the industry. Introduction, in 1925, of the factory ship, with a stern ramp for easy loading and processing of giant rorquals, made massacres virtually inevitable. Over the next five years, the number of factory ships rose to 41 and a total of more than 75,000 blue whales alone were killed.

Currently, there are not enough large whales available to make whaling economically viable. Minke whales *(Balaenoptera acutorostrata)*, which grow no more than 33.5 feet long and weigh 11 tons, have been the mainstay of modern whaling. Most of the International Whaling Commission's 41 member states no longer whale. Even the Soviet Union mothballed most of its whaling fleet in 1987. IWC members are observing a five year moratorium on commercial whaling that ends in 1990, though it may be renewed. This did not prevent Japan and Iceland from taking hundreds of whales--most were minkes, but they included fins and seis *(Balaenoptera borealis)*--in 1987 and 1988, claiming these were sacrificed for scientific purposes, as allowed by IWC rules.

The present collapse of commercial whaling, rough as it may be on whalers and their families, is too late for the hundreds of thousands of whales that have died as the giant factory ships swallowed increasingly smaller species. It does mean that the specter of biological extinction for some cetacean species has slowed its dreadful march. But whales, dolphins and porpoises are still dying because of human activities, and the toll surpasses 100,000 each year, according to the IWC.

~

Subsistence Whaling

Besides the continuing hemorrhage of whale lives through loopholes in the commercial whaling ban and the outlaw activities of a few pirate whalers, hunting is permitted on a subsistence basis. For the Alaskan Inupiat Eskimos, this means that the United States acknowledges the importance of the bowhead to traditional culture, which is fast blending into a money economy. Under IWC quotas, the Inupiats can take up to 26 bowheads each year, nearly three times their average kill between 1912 and 1967.

This places unwise pressure on the rare bowhead, which is believed to number no more than 4,400 and is one of the world's most endangered whales. However, the Inupiats have steadfastly resisted switching the hunt to grays or any other available whale. Former bowhead hunters in eastern Siberia did switch to the gray in 1930. The IWC allows Soviet whalers to catch about 180 annually for the aborigines, though reports persist that much of this meat detours into the gullets of foxes and minks on fur farms.

Other aboriginal whale hunts include those of the Inuit Eskimos of western Greenland and eastern Canada, which had an IWC quota of 220 minkes and 10 fins for the two years ending in 1987. These native peoples account for an estimated 1,000 beluga and narwhal kills each year and unknown numbers of pilot whale kills. Residents of the Danish Faroe Islands, located halfway between Scotland and Iceland, conduct a drive fishery that forces pilot whales ashore where an estimated 1,000 a year are gaffed and killed with lances and knives.

Natives of two island groups in the North Atlantic, the Portuguese-owned Azores and Madeira, had gone after sperm whales since being taught how by Yankee whalers in the mid-1800s. Both have recently ceased whaling, and Madeira has declared its coast a marine mammal sanctuary.

~

The Incidental Toll

A prime cause of cetacean mortality today is the incidental killing of dolphins and porpoises in the nets of various fisheries. Deep-water spinner (*Stenella longirostris*) and spotted (*Stenella attenuata*) dolphins often swim with yellowfin tuna in the tropical Pacific. Huge tuna seiners set their nets on the mammals to capture the fish beneath and in the process thousands drown, though fishermen may make extraordinary efforts to free the dolphins. Between 1960, when tuna fishermen switched from hooks to purse seines, and 1975 an estimated three to five million dolphins were killed in the nets. This "incidental take" of spotted, spinner, and other dolphins became so common that some animals learned to dive deep enough to avoid the net before it closed. Other predators, such as the false killer whale (*Pseudorca crassidens*) and the pygmy killer whale (*Feresa attenuata*), associated the sounds of a net with exhausted dolphins, which made for easy meals. Their opportunistic hunting overturned the belief that only orcas ate other marine mammals.

After years of argument and experiment on ways to reduce the incidental toll, in 1984 the U.S. Congress established a quota of no more than 20,500 dolphin deaths annually. Once that number is reached, the American fleet must stop fishing on porpoise, as the technique is known. Onboard observers from the National Marine Fisheries Service and stiff fines for violators give the law real teeth.

Another dozen nations field tuna fleets, and their captains are not bound by U.S. laws. However, some countries are starting to require procedures that save dolphin lives. Mexico is fielding observers on selected boats to beef up enforcement of its laws.

Using gill nets to catch salmon offshore, Japanese fishermen incidentally killed an estimated 10,000 to 20,000 Dall's porpoises annually in the 1970s. Quotas were imposed for gill net fishing in U.S. controlled waters, and that figure dropped to an estimated 741 porpoises in 1987. But gill nets continue to entangle and drown cetaceans, especially young ones. An increase in cod fishing off Newfoundland, Canada, succeeded in trapping young humpbacks as well as fish. At one time or another, most coastal cetacean species end up in gill nets--especially the nets constructed of nylon monofilament strands. These nets are not only more durable than the ones made of natural fibers, but they also appear harder to detect even if the whale has echolocation.

Another man-made hazard is the growing amount of plastic debris in the oceans. Cetaceans are among the victims of the estimated 350 million pounds of nonbiodegradable materials lost or dumped into the ocean each year by merchant and passenger ships as well as fishing vessels. An autopsy of a minke that stranded on a Texas beach in 1988 revealed plastic sheets in three of the whale's four stomachs. Like sea turtles, the whales that swallow plastic may think they are eating salps or sea combs, the translucent organisms belonging to the jellyfish family.

~

Attacking the Support System

As obviously lethal as is the slaying of whales and dolphins, incidental to fishing or otherwise, it is the ongoing destruction of their ecological support systems that poses the gravest danger in the long run. Freshwater river dolphins are among the species most threatened by loss of natural habitat. Hydroelectric dams and development along its limited riverline home bode ill for the Ganges or blind river dolphin (*Platanista gangetica*) of India, Nepal and Bangladesh. The boto, or Amazon River, dolphin (*Inia geoffrensis*) has the misfortune to live in Brazil's major aquatic artery, one that bears the brunt of the Amazon basin's extensive deforestation. Brazil has even announced plans to dam the mighty Amazon itself.

In the Antarctic, half a dozen nations compete with the surviving rorquals for the krill. This shrimplike crustacean is processed into a food paste. The 1986/87 krill harvest amounted to 376,527 metric tons; it has ranged as high as 528,000 metric tons in a season. Scientists are still not able to predict accurately the total productivity of the region, so assessing the impact of krill harvesting is haphazard. Holes in the atmospheric ozone layer, which may damage plankton reproduction, add yet another element of unpredictability to understanding changes in the southern ocean's crucial ecosystems.

With industrial and urban wastes joining agricultural

runoffs into the world's rivers and oceans, coastal seas are becoming more noxious with each passing year. The resulting accumulation of toxic chemicals and metals in their bodies is likely to prove devastating to cetaceans. As top predators in several aquatic food webs, whales concentrate pollutants like DDT, PCBs and mercury in their organs and tissues when the fish, squid, or krill they consume contain these toxic substances. The smaller organisms, in turn, have distilled the poisons from their prey, so each level of feeding has produced a larger dose of contaminants. Some toxins are expelled through a cetacean's normal excretions, including mother's milk, but varying amounts remain bound to the blubber or to organs like the brain, liver and kidneys.

Though the first evidence that cetaceans carried toxic pollutants in their flesh was published in 1967, there is still little more than a fragmentary picture of the problem. Not all whale species have been analyzed for chlorinated hydrocarbons, like DDT; heavy metals, such as mercury; or petroleum-based hydrocarbons and sometimes the data collected may be flawed by the complexity of the animals examined. For instance, a study of harbor porpoises (Phocoena phocoena) in Canada's Bay of Fundy indicated that DDT in blubber rose 50 to 3000 percent in males as they grew older. But DDT levels in females dropped after age four, when they reached sexual maturity. The likely, and disturbing, reason is that the pesticide was passed to their fetuses and, during nursing, to calves.

Baleen whales seem to have the lowest levels of general toxicity, perhaps due to relatively unpolluted polar feeding grounds. A few baleens, primarily fins, taken in urbanized coastal waters off France and eastern Canada have had higher pesticide concentrations than those from the Antarctic. Another baleen with a high degree of contamination is the gray, the only whale that regularly feeds off coastal seabeds.

In the case of many toothed whales, coastal home ranges, frequent exposure to industrial and urban wastes, and diets relying on bottomfish or squid contribute to extremely heavy contamination. Coastal populations of harbor porpoises are widely considered in decline, and the Council of Europe has proclaimed the animal "endangered by pollution."

The saltwater St. Lawrence River estuary in Quebec province is within Canada's most populated and industrialized region and is home to over 400 belugas. Between 1983 and 1988, at least 88 white whale carcasses laden with toxic chemicals washed ashore. Biologist Pierre Beland of the St. Lawrence National Institute of Ecotoxicology noted that the dead whales were so contaminated that technically they should have been considered toxic waste.

Such high levels of neurotoxic mercury were found in beluga meat in the 1960s that by 1970 Canada ceased hunting the whales commercially. That did not mean the killing (or consumption) stopped completely. Subsistence hunting by Eskimos in the Canadian Arctic apparently continued, as did the Soviet beluga hunt. This is strange in light of Japan's experience with the mercury poisoning of thousands of people in and around Minamata who ate local fish tainted by industrial waste.

Often there are no clearly definable causes for whale deaths. Such is the case in the largest cetacean die-off in recent U.S history. The epidemic deposited at least 800 bottlenose dolphin corpses along the Eastern seaboard between June 1987 and February 1988. Autopsies documented a wide variety of bacterial infections that could cause pneumonia, cerebral hemorrhage, shock, or vasuclar collapse. Some, but not all, bodies analyzed contained toxic levels of chlorinated hydrocarbons.

The chief investigator, wildlife disease expert Dr. Joseph Geraci, said most industrial pollutants have been ruled out and the culprit may be a natural poison. He linked the dolphin die-off with marine changes that produced a rare "red tide" along the East Coast in November 1987. Dr. Geraci stopped short of blaming the deaths on toxins released by the microscopic organisms whose swarms turn the sea brick red. For one thing, the timing was wrong for the initial dolphin casualties. But there may have been an underlying chain reaction that linked the events together.

Another separate series of baleen whale deaths off Cape Cod during the end of 1987 and beginning of 1988 has been tied to a biotoxin. About a dozen humpbacks, two fins, and a minke died before investigators pinpointed the poison in the organs of mackerel. The fish was temporarily banned for human consumption in Massachusetts. So far there is no explanation of why the mackerel suddenly became toxic, but this may herald ominous changes.

~

Mass Strandings

While individuals of virtually all known species of large and small whales have washed ashore at one time or another --this may be the only evidence that some of them exist-- odontocetes seem far more prone to strand en masse than baleen whales. The species most commonly associated with live mass strandings are both the long-finned (Globicephala melaena) and short-finned (Globicephala macrohynchus) pilot whales and the false killer whale. They may beach themselves in groups ranging from a half-dozen to hundreds.

The largest reported stranding among the three species

is of an estimated 835 false killer whales that inundated the Atlantic resort beaches around Mar del Plata, Argentina, in 1946. Such a high figure is questionable, partly because herds of the false killer whale in this quantity have never before been reported. However, there are well documented strandings involving between 100 and 300 false killers on beaches ranging from Australia to Scotland during a 50-year period. Pilot whale herds of up to 200 animals have beached on the shores of Newfoundland. All three of these dolphins, which grow to 20 feet in length, are usually found well offshore in tropical and temperate waters, though they migrate seasonally to coastal zones. Coastal residents, like the harbor porpoise and bottlenose dolphin, frequently strand individually, but most single live strandings can be attributed to injury, disease, or parasitic infections.

What causes mass strandings is one of the most perplexing questions pursued by whale researchers. Most mass stranders dwell offshore and live in large social groups. It has been suggested that they follow prey, or are chased by predators like sharks and orcas, into unfamiliar shallows and ground on gently sloping beaches that misdirect their echolocation signals. Parasites in the whales' middle ears have been blamed for mass strandings, as has the tendency of herds to follow their leaders.

The problem is that no theoretical cause fits all existing facts surrounding stranded groups. Most autopsied animals have little or nothing in their stomachs, undercutting one plausible reason for being so close to shore. Cetaceans abound in parasites, but no organism has yet been linked to stranding behavior. Evidence for a herd following an ill leader onto a beach is fragmentary at best and falls apart when the stranding takes place over miles of beach and a period of days. Even orcas and sperm whales are known to mass strand--56 mostly male sperm whales beached in Baja California in January 1979; another 41 did it six months later near Florence, Oregon--so it is unlikely they were panicked by a predator.

~

Mysteries to Come

Cetacean research is a relatively recent field of scientific study, even if Aristotle started the ball rolling 2,400 years ago by firmly declaring whales to be mammals rather than fish. As a new science concerned with animals that are hard to observe and have, in many species, been hunted into near-oblivion, it often raises more questions than it answers. Witness the uncertainty over echolocation in baleens and the use of sound to kill prey by toothed whales; the unknown impact of marine pollution and the enigma of mass strandings. These indicate the whale's potential to stir our curiosity and hint at mysteries yet to come.

The more we learn about these awesome animals, the greater our interest in keeping whales alive, both for themselves and to reveal the water world we share. Whalewatching, though seasonal, has become a multimillion-dollar business on the east and west coasts of the U.S. Hundreds of thousands of hopeful whalewatchers take two to three hour trips from ports along the migratory routes of grays or to the feeding and mating grounds of humpbacks. And they are frequently rewarded with dolphins hitching a ride on a bow wave or, less often, incredible displays of breaching, spyhopping or lunge-feeding.

In fact, watching live whales has grown so popular that it has had to be restricted in some areas, such as Alaska's Glacier Bay or off Maui, Hawaii, to avoid harassing the whales. Mexico made one of the grays' nursery lagoons a sanctuary in 1971 and strictly limits the number of tour boats. However, even with noise pollution and possible harassment by boaters, whalewatching is a far better use of whales, if humans must use them, than the uses derived from the dead animals. With the possible exception of cultures where identity may be intertwined with whaling, there are no uses for dead whales for which a substitute product is not already available.

Our fascination with whales shows up in circular debates over their intelligence as well as heroic roles in popular films and literature. For some they epitomize a broken pact for peaceful co-existence with nature; to others they represent a lost innocence, a natural unity, that may never have existed; and yet others see them as an inane romanticism that threatens to hold back human progress, which is usually defined in terms of growth and struggle against nature. In the process, the reality of whales living in their own realm, gracefully adapted citizens of the global sea, too easily escapes notice. Yet their beauty exists for all to share.

Hopefully the best is yet to come. As we watch and learn from live whales, we can shape a more humane ethic for living with others different from ourselves. We may regain an appreciation of life's interconnectedness that seems to have wilted in the process of building concrete and steel cocoons to further human dominion. If such an ethic spreads quickly enough, saving whales may save ourselves and we might yet mature into stewards of the planet, rather than its putative masters.

~

Previous Page: Lunging out of the water is called "breaching." *This Page:* Throat grooves aid the gray in suction feeding on tiny crustaceans living in the top layer of the sea floor. *Facing Page:* White splotches like these on a gray whale are usually scar tissue from barnacle clusters that have fallen or been rubbed off. Since the skin slowly regains its gray tone, these discolorations give the adult a mottled appearance.

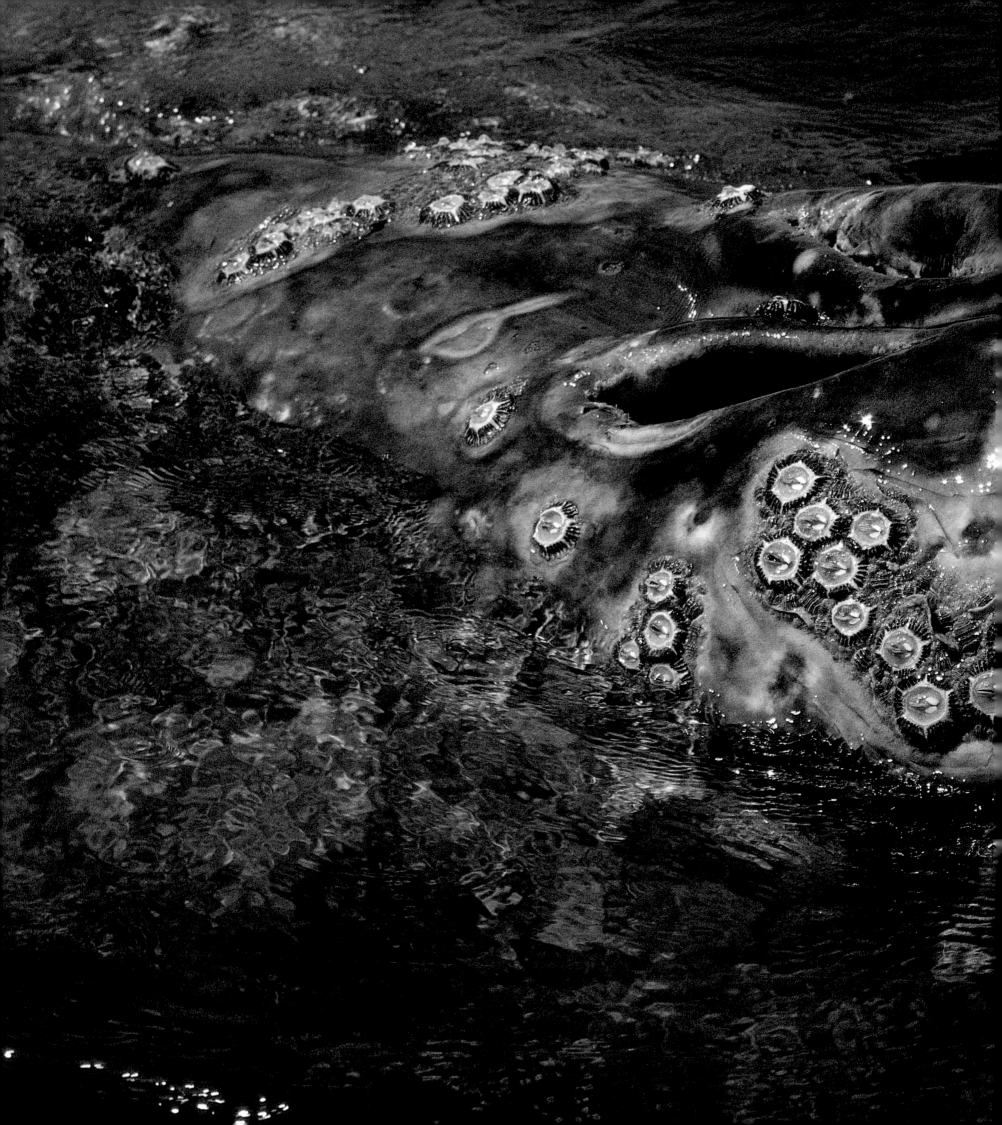

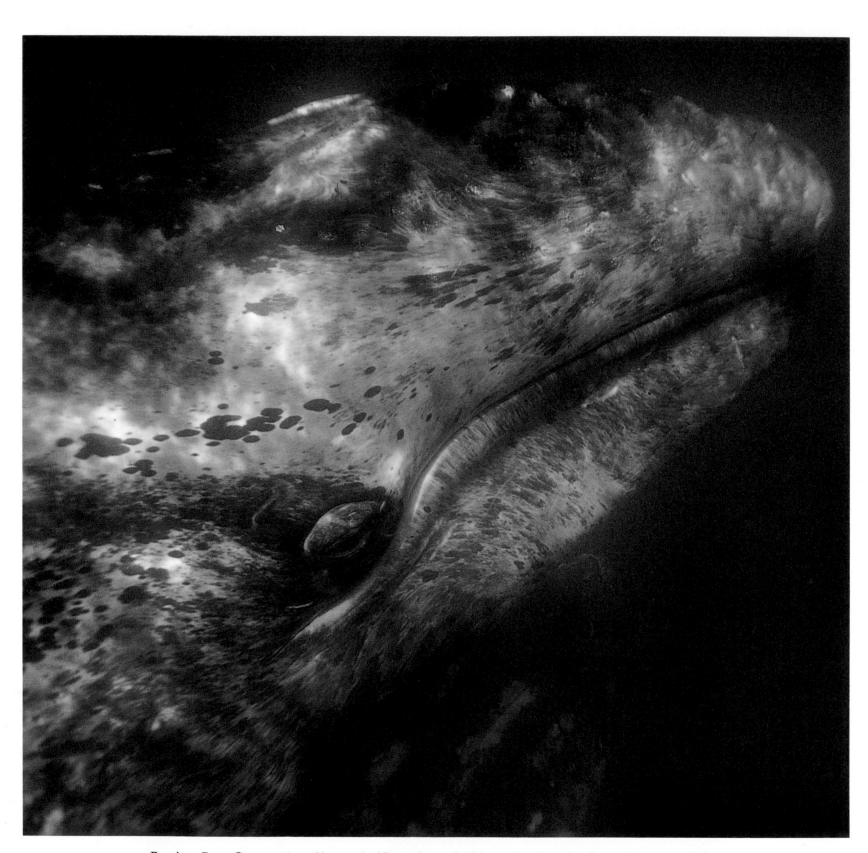

Previous Page: One species of barnacle *(Cryptolepas rhachianecti)* is found only on the gray whale.
Barnacles are also filter-feeders. By attaching to the whale, they dine on the oceans' richest fare with
a mobility that must be the envy of the crustacean world. *This Page:* A gray whale calf—this one is
obviously too recently born to have acquired any barnacles—swims near the surface of a lagoon in
Baja California, Mexico. *Facing Page:* An adult gray brings her calf to a skiff in a Baja California lagoon for a pat. She is one of a number of grays nicknamed "the friendlies."

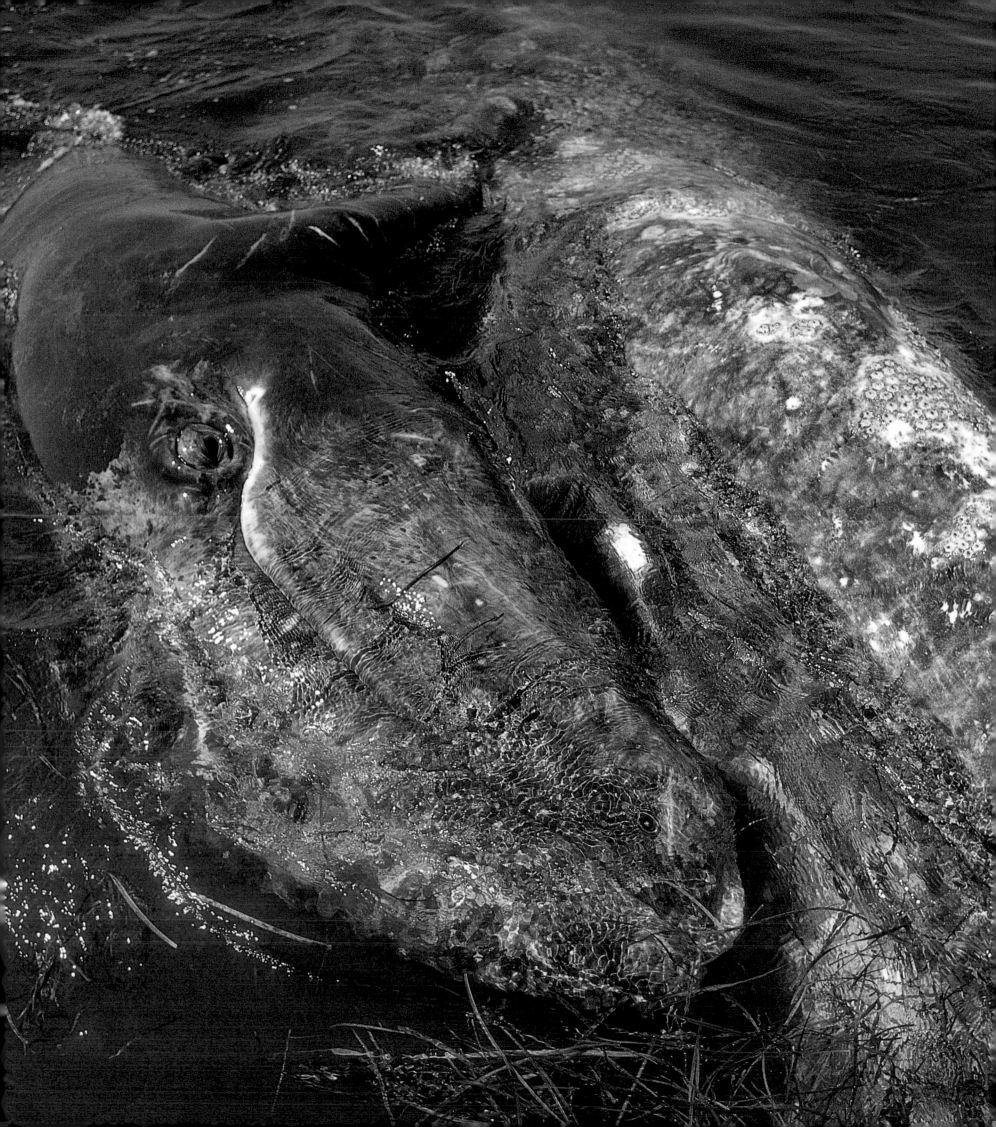

This Page: A young gray whale swims alone in a lagoon at Baja California, Mexico. *Facing Page:* Surrounding the clusters of whale barnacles on grays are no fewer than three species of whale lice, a parasitic crustacean that quickly spreads to all parts of the whale's body.

This Page: A blue whale's spout, or blow, can rise to 30 feet and is a distinctively narrow column of water vapor. The blue whale's numbers have been severely reduced by overhunting. *Facing Page:* In normal swimming, blues probably do not dive deeply because their principal food lives in the top 330 feet of the ocean. They may weigh as much as 150 tons, but for all their bulk, they depend on essentially one type of prey, krill.

This Page: The tail of the blue whale plays host to dark remora fish known as "whalesuckers." Although they attach themselves to cetaceans for a free ride, they are not parasites. *Facing Page:* Though adult blues are thought too large to breach, that does not stop this calf from showing the oldsters how it is done. It was 24 feet long when born and weighed between 2.5 and 3 tons.

Facing Page: A broad rostrum with a central ridge running up to the nostrils and two smaller, parallel ridges are the Bryde's most distinctive feature. Otherwise, it closely resembles the larger sei whale, which is another rorqual. *This Page:* A mother Bryde's whale and calf flash the dark, sickle-shaped dorsal fin that appears two-thirds of the way down the animal's back. At birth, the calf is about 11 feet long; an adult female may reach 45 feet.

This Page: Captive belugas, which aquaria have only learned to maintain since 1961, are our main sources of biological information on this species. *Facing Page:* Both young belugas and narwhals, to which they are closely related, start life with a dark gray color, but by the sixth year the beluga is creamy white. It eats large fish, like cod and flounder, and small ones, like capelin.

Previous Page: Belugas are the social butterflies of the Arctic and have been reported in big herds ranging from 500 in the Saint Lawrence River to over 10,000 in the Western Hudson Bay. Solitary whales have been seen as far south as Avalon, New Jersey. In 1966, one swam 250 miles up the Rhine in West Germany. *This Page:* The dorsal feature that gives the fin whale its common name is up to two feet tall and curved like a sickle. The whale is also known as the "finback" or "razorback." *Facing Page:* The most streamlined of the rorquals, the fin whale has a maximum speed of slightly above 25 miles per hour. It is slower than the blue whale, though it may have greater endurance. *Overleaf:* A mother whale escorting her calf. The calf is born in temperate waters where it nurses until it is six months old. In early summer the whales resume their feeding in cold water regions.

This Page: Humpback whales are among the most acrobatic of the great whales, and appear to enjoy breaching. This kind of behavior is what draws tourists to whale-watching off the East Coast. Naturalists are concerned about whale-watching boats disturbing the whales. *Facing Page:* Lobtailing, or smashing the surface with its flukes, is one kind of exuberant humpback behavior that is not really understood. The best guess is that it is either an acoustic signal to other whales, or, if associated with feeding, that it may stun potential prey.

This Page: When preparing to dive deeply, or "sound," the humpback lowers its head and arches its spine, accentuating the humped appearance. *Facing Page:* To execute a breach, as this humpback is doing off the coast of Hawaii, the whale first builds momentum by swimming underwater parallel to the surface. Then it must lift a weight equivalent to 485 people.

Facing Page: A minke tips the scales at over 11 tons, but its spout is quick and inconspicuous on the ocean. It is a highly migratory animal, often travelling to find food. Minkes have been known to enter the ice fields in order to feed. *This Page:* Once known as the "little piked whales," minkes in the northern hemisphere have a unique white patch on the top side of their flippers and creamy white baleen. Southern ocean subspecies wear different color patterns.

This Page: A native of Arctic seas, the narwhal is a 15 foot animal with one tooth—its horn. Males grow a spiral tooth up to 9 feet long, however, it is rare for females to produce such a tusk. *Facing Page:* Found in subpolar regions as well as in temperate waters, the right whale presented whalers with a slow-swimming, easy-to-kill target that floated when dead. Hence the name "right" whale.

Facing Page: Rolling in the waves off Nova Scotia, a black right whale shows the white marking on its belly and its broad, flat flippers. *This Page:* As the calf nestles against its mother the white patch on the underside of the mother is clearly visible. The patch has led to the nickname of "whitebelly."

Facing Page: Blainville's beaked whale, also called the dense-beaked whale, is not known to exceed 17 feet in length and is mostly found in the tropics on both sides of the equator. *This Page:* The adult male Blainville's has a scooplike lower jaw that supports a tooth on either side. This is an unusual tooth location even among the rare beaked whales, but it probably has little funtional value. Beaked whales feed mainly on squid, which they swallow whole.

This Page: Orcas are found all over the world. One of the densest populations is in the straits off Vancouver Island, British Columbia, where this animal was photographed. *Facing Page:* Spyhopping allows the orca to use its excellent eyesight out of water. In oceanaria shows, captive orcas prove their visual acuity with tricks, like leaping for hand held fish.

Facing Page: A lone orca swims in Mc Murdo's Sound, Antartica, in search of food. *This Page:* This group of orcas are sleeping. Whales are the most specialized of all marine mammals. They spend all their life in water whereas other sea animals, such as seals, return to land at frequent intervals.

This Page: Breaching orcas may leap fully out of water in the wild, a behavior that can be trained so that they leap on command in captivity. As they are the largest members of the dolphin family, this makes quite a spectacular show. *Facing Page:* Pulsed sounds, clicks and vocalizations by hunting orcas may be mixed with tail slaps, lunging and splashing to help drive and corral prey. They are avid predators, feeding on fish, squid and other marine mammals.

Facing Page: Mature bull orcas can be identified by their large, paddle-shaped flippers. A 30-foot male that stranded in Scotland had flippers over 6.5 feet long and 3.5 feet wide. *This Page:* Regional killer whale pods have distinct vocalizations, which have been labelled "dialects," that are believed to contribute to group identity and cohesion.

These Pages: These two orcas swim alone. However, groups or "pods" ranging from three to more than twenty animals have been studied, with strong matriarchal ties observed. Offspring often swim with their mothers long after weaning—for ten years in one recorded case.

Facing Page: Up to 26 pairs of teeth on each jaw equip the bottlenose to hold and swallow mullet, catfish, squid, eels and just about anything else it can catch. In the ocean, these open jaws would be a threatening gesture. *This Page:* Bottlenoses at sea often leap out of water as they swim, a maneuver called "porpoising." They can reach speeds of 16 miles an hour. Though wary and difficult to capture, bottlenoses readily adapt to confinement and human contact. Friendly and tractable, they lend themselves to experiments that are slowly identifying dolphin ability and behavior.

This Page: With a rearward glance, this bottlenose is possibly trying to coordinate movements with the rough-toothed dolphins with which it swims. Bottlenoses often mix with other dolphin species, even mating with some, including the rough-toothed. *Facing Page:* Many different dolphin species have been reported at play in the wild and, without prior training, in captivity. Bottlenoses often exhibit energetic exuberance and creativity at play.

This Page: These black-and-white dolphins eat squid and various deep-dwelling fish known to rise to-ward the surface at night. Little is known about the right whale dolphin's diving ability. *Facing Page:* Found in temperate and tropical open seas, the spinner dolphin is one of the smaller members of the dolphin family. Its name describes the unique movement of spinning as it leaps through the air.

Facing Page: The Pacific white-sided dolphin is a playful sea mammal with the ability to jump high. It grows to be between 7 and 8 feet long and can weigh over 300 pounds. *This Page:* Pacific white-sided dolphins are gregarious, and aggregate herds of 1,000 are not uncommon. They will also swim with mixed herds of striped, common and northern right whale dolphins.

Facing Page: Risso's dolphin, which was named after a French naturalist, usually travels in groups of around 50, but may be seen as a single animal or in herds of several hundred. It ranges throughout the world's temperate and tropical waters. *This Page:* Not much is known about wild rough-toothed dolphins except they are usually found in warm waters and do not often strand. Captive dolphins easily dive to 150 feet and, once tame, are trainable for complex tasks. The first hybrid off-spring produced in captivity was the result of mating rough-toothed dolphins with bottlenoses.

Facing Page: Spotted dolphins are known to echolocate and each is believed to have its own identification sound, a "signature whistle." The "melon," or forehead area, focuses the sound beams. *This Page:* Often confused with the common dolphin, the striped dolphin is longer, reaching 10 feet, and weighs 250 pounds. A blue-black stripe runs from the eyes along the flanks to the anal region.

This Page: Certain Atlantic spotted dolphin populations frequent Florida's coastline, though they are usually found well offshore in both temperate and tropical waters. *Facing Page:* The Atlantic spotted dolphin is similar to the bottlenose but is 3 to 5 feet shorter and can be easily distinguished by its markings.

This Page: The boutu or Amazon River dolphin is the largest of the four freshwater dolphin species. It grows to be just under 10 feet long and weighs 200 pounds, changing color from gray to pink as it matures. Though the freshwater dolphins are considered more primitive than their marine cousins, the boutu is trainable and has a brain-body ratio close to that of the bottlenose dolphin. *Facing Page:* Dusky dolphins are social animals and are among the few wild cetaceans known to do somersaults. Such acrobatics probably communicate prey location information to others and might express a joyful mood.